MW01109355

THE SINGLE MAN'S
HOUSECLEANING
PLAYBOOK

A quick and simple guide to cleaning your
home like a pro

SIDNEY SHOWALTER

authorHOUSE®

AuthorHouse™ LLC
1663 Liberty Drive
Bloomington, IN 47403
www.authorhouse.com
Phone: 1-800-839-8640

© 2014 Sidney Showalter. All rights reserved.

No part of this book may be reproduced, stored in a retrieval system, or transmitted by any means without the written permission of the author.

Published by AuthorHouse   07/21/2014

ISBN: 978-1-4969-1391-3 (sc)
ISBN: 978-1-4969-1390-6 (hc)
ISBN: 978-1-4969-1389-0 (e)

Library of Congress Control Number: 2014909272

Any people depicted in stock imagery provided by Thinkstock are models, and such images are being used for illustrative purposes only. Certain stock imagery © Thinkstock.

This book is printed on acid-free paper.

Because of the dynamic nature of the Internet, any web addresses or links contained in this book may have changed since publication and may no longer be valid. The views expressed in this work are solely those of the author and do not necessarily reflect the views of the publisher, and the publisher hereby disclaims any responsibility for them.

Contents

SPECIAL PLAYS

Acknowledgments

Thanks to Uncle Ed Whitcomb, my inspiration for writing a book, and Cousin Rosemary Messick for her encouragement and support from the inception through the publication of the book. Others include Pat Reynolds, my housecleaning coach who shared her cleaning knowledge with me, Lisa Wrobley, a professor at Florida Gulf Coast University, for early guidance, Judy Edwards and Alice Fraser for editing in the early stages, Judith Dallal, Diane Sebass, Maria Davis, and my sisters, Susan Showalter and "Baby Seester" Sarah Klatt, for their help in the latter stages. I would also like to thank Dave Tanner for lending me his football playbook and Naples High School for the helmet and use of the field.

A special thank-you goes to Robert Berman, my very good friend here in Naples, for editing and marketing ideas, and to Kelly Cahill of AuthorHouse Publishing, who held my hand from the beginning to the completion of the publishing process.

Preface

One day my house cleaner, Ruth, called me to tell me that she had broken her arm and would not be working for six weeks. I had two choices—hire a new house cleaner or do it myself. Ruth had always done a fabulous job cleaning my house; therefore, I wanted her to return as soon as possible. Recently retired, I decided I would give it a go myself. Not knowing what I was getting myself into, I thought cleaning would be no big deal.

I had little training or experience with housecleaning. My mom had made me make my bed and take out the trash. (She also made me feed the dog and bring in the paper.) My dad, a retired judge with lots of time on his hands, became an expert at using the vacuum cleaner. At Boys Club Camp I had to make my bed in such a manner that a quarter would bounce on it, put my clothes in a drawer, and sweep the floor and porch. As a college fraternity pledge, I performed various jobs to keep our house clean. When I was a waiter, I learned how to set and clean tables and wash pots and pans. The first month at Navy Officers Candidate School (OCS) I shared responsibilities for keeping the barracks clean. In all these instances I did tasks I thought I would never do again.

After a few weeks of housecleaning, I began to get the hang of it. I learned to do tasks correctly in the proper sequence, and by trial and error, I learned what products to use. I also gained knowledge from speaking with housewives and women who cleaned professionally.

Besides personal experience of trial and error and talking and working with house cleaners, I also did a little research by reading other books on cleaning. One day, while doing my research, I walked into a major bookstore and asked to see the housecleaning section. The male sales assistant asked me what I was looking for. When I told him that I was writing a book, he casually asked me what it was about. When I replied that the title was the *Single Man's Housecleaning Playbook*, he burst out laughing and remarked that he had never heard of a book like that before. I was delighted! After I looked through the bookcases, explored Amazon, and checked the library, I began to realize that I couldn't find a book that was similar to what I had in mind.

I began to realize that most men (and maybe a lot of women) have never been taught much about how to clean a house. Our mothers gave us some guidance and instruction, but unless we took home economics, we were left to fend for ourselves. I realized that a book like I had in mind could benefit a great number of people and save them a lot of time. It was at that point I decided to give it a try. My objective was to write a book that explained all of the basics:

- what to do
- how to do it
- what to do it with
- when to do it

I decided my book would be patterned after a football playbook that house cleaners could refer to when they needed to keep themselves on the right route. I also realized that a subject like this might be quite boring, so I tried to lighten the story up with a little trivia and humor to keep the reader from falling to sleep.

After several years of procrastinating, with prodding by my cousin Dr. Rosemary Messsick, I have finished the book. I hope it will be of benefit to you.

THE STORY

Chapter 1

THE MASTER BEDROOM

I wish I could say that the 7:00 a.m. alarm woke me out of a sound sleep, but I can't. To quote an old song, "I didn't sleep at all last night!" It's not unusual for an athlete the night before a big game to stay awake all night. Today my big game is coming up with a plan on how to clean my home in a quick and efficient manner so that I will have more time to play golf and go out sailing on the Gulf of Mexico.

I have tried many house cleaners, but they never seem to work out. When the last one broke her arm, I decided to tackle the job myself. *Why?* Because it seemed like it shouldn't be so hard—do a little dusting, wash a few windows, pick up some clutter lying around, and run the sweeper. *What's so hard about that?* I didn't know, but I was about to find out.

As I lay there in the bed, many questions arose. How long it would take? How would I attack the situation? What cleaning materials would I need? Where should I start? What was I getting myself into?

Then I had a brainstorm! Cleaning a house is just like playing football. No matter what position you play, you have to know what to do, how to do it, and when to do it. I thought that if I figured out the techniques, how to execute them, and when to implement them, maybe I could make the job more efficient—quick and easy. The process could be a game and a challenge instead of a dreaded task.

Fortunately there are a few things that my mother had continually preached to me that made my life easier. I can hear her now!

- "Make your bed when you get up. Then you won't have to remember to do it later, and your room will look a lot neater."
- "When you get done using something, put it back where it belongs so someone else can find it."
- "When you take off your clothes, put them in the hamper or hang them up so someone else doesn't have to pick up after you or step over them."

I used to get really upset about her nagging, but she said it would pay off later in life. I now live alone, and there isn't a wife or mother to pick up after me. What I realized after I had written this book was that my mother was my first coach. She taught me the basics of all the different positions, how to execute the maneuvers, and when to put them into action. Now I would hear her say,

- "Every time you make your bed, you will get better at it and able to do it more quickly. Practice, practice, practice!"
- "Putting things back after using them is just like returning the weights to their proper place in the workout room."
- "Put your uniform back in the locker or throw it in the hamper."

Garrison Keillor's stories of Norwegian bachelors living as slobs and the stereotypes in movies about men living in messes don't fit a lot of us guys. As a matter of fact, a lot of my single male friends have very presentable homes. The conception that single males are slobs isn't always true.

Coming back to the job facing me, I continued to think. The right place to start would be right here. I was lying here in my bed. It had to be made, and the sheets needed to be changed. I thought, *Brilliant! When I get up, I will just strip the bed, put on clean sheets, and finish with the bedspread.*

So I jumped out of the bed, ripped off the pillowcases, threw the bedspread on the floor, and stripped the sheets off the bed. I got fresh sheets from the linen closet, put on the fitted sheet and the flat sheet, picked up the bedspread, and put it back on the bed.

Damned fitted sheets!

I folded back the bedspread, put the fresh cases on the pillows, put the pillows on the bed, and neatly pulled the bedspread up over the pillows. I was finished. *Wow!* I thought. *My first series of plays are completed, and it probably took less than five minutes! This will be a snap!*

Okay, what else needs to be done to clean up this room? Firstly pants, shirt, and shoes need to be picked up and put away, and the carpet needs to be vacuumed. Furniture needs to be dusted, and the mirrors and windows should be cleaned.

That's not so hard.

I picked my pants and shirt, put my shoes in the closet, and threw my socks and underwear in the hamper. Next I got out the vacuum, pushed it around the room, grabbed a cloth, and dusted the furniture. I was proud of myself because I was picking off these jobs like a linebacker intercepting passes. "Oh crap! Penalty," I said as I noticed my footprints in the freshly vacuumed carpet. After I ran the vacuum again, I noticed that I needed to clean the windows and mirrors, so I got the Windex and did the windows and mirror. Yep, you guessed it. Another big penalty this time because I messed up the carpet again and spotted up the freshly dusted dresser. Fifteen yards and loss of down! I dusted the dresser again and vacuumed the carpet again.

After I finished vacuuming the carpet for the third time and looked at the streaks on the windows and mirrors and lint on the freshly dusted dressers, I realized that I needed to reevaluate the sequence of my plays or punt.

Maybe this isn't as easy as I thought. At that point I realized my sequence of doing the jobs right and in the proper sequence was paramount so that I wasn't messing up something I had already done. Since I didn't have a mentor or coach, I needed to develop my own playbook.

Okay, I thought. *If doing the mirrors leaves spray and mist spots on the furniture and walking around and dusting leaves footprints on the carpet, I need to change the sequence.* I decided that I should work in the following order:

1. Clean windows and mirrors and any other glass.
2. Dust.
3. Vacuum.

I had my sequence for cleaning the bedroom in order, but there were still a few glitches that needed to be straightened out.

What about the streaky mirrors and windows? If you want, you can buy commercial window sprays. The only problem is that they often contain ammonia, which can harm solar coatings on the windows. I have a friend that installs solar film. He uses a spray bottle full of liquid dishwashing soap, vinegar, and water and scrubs them down with a rag or soft brush. Then he uses a squeegee to finish it off, and he wipes off the corners with a clean paper towel or newspaper. I discovered that if you look at the windows or mirrors from a side angle, you can see the streaks or film left after you have dried them off.

Another trick I learned after spraying and washing the window is to run my hand over the glass because I can feel tiny specks that I sometimes can't see; When my hand starts to vibrate as I move it across the window, I know that it is clean. As Andy Rooney might have said, "Streaky windows and mirrors bug me."

What about dusting? Sometimes I have used a dry cloth. Sometimes I have used a damp cloth, but a damp cloth probably isn't good for wood if I use it on a constant basis. Probably the best thing I have used is a clean rag like a hand towel that doesn't have lint and furniture dusting spray on a limited basis. For big flat surfaces I sometimes use furniture spray and make sure to wipe it dry. For chair rounds and other similar places I spray the cloth and wipe them clean and dry. If you really want to do an outstanding job, use the microfiber cloths.

Then there are the items that have crevices that a dust cloth won't get into. That's the place for a vacuum hose with brush attachment on the end. It lends a clean, professional look.

One thing I noticed the second time I went through the process were the places I had missed and everyone else seems to miss too—the baseboard, above the windows and door frames, panels in the wooden doors, and ceiling fans. Luckily I can stand on my bed and reach the top of the ceiling fan when I need to clean it. One thing you have to remember is to spread something on the bed to catch the dust if the fan is directly above it. I am also tall enough to reach the top of the door frames and windows.

Bending over isn't that difficult to do when dusting the baseboards. After all, quarterbacks bend over or squat all the time. Baseboards and fans don't have to be done every time you clean, but once a month is about right.

Oh, yes, you might have to do the lamp shades. If the sides are flat, you can usually wipe them off with a dust or microfiber cloth. However, if the shades are pleated as mine are, the brush on the hose from the vacuum cleaner does a fine job. Just don't forget to dust the light and inside the shade.

I took a look around and said to myself, "Not bad! The bed is made. Everything has been picked up. The mirrors are clean. The furniture has been dusted, and the carpet has been vacuumed. I may not have done it in the right sequence the first or second time, but now I know, and it will be a lot easier the next time."

When I timed myself, I found that I could change the bed in about four minutes. Cleaning the three double-hung windows and two mirrors takes about five minutes. Dusting takes about seven minutes. That includes the headboard, two nightstands, a double-wide dresser, a tall dresser, and two straight-back chairs. I discovered that the fewer items I have to move around to dust, the faster the job goes. Speed depends on two things—how dirty the place is and how efficient you are at dusting.

If you look at a model home or picture in a magazine, you will find that they have only a few items placed on top of the furniture. They are usually placed for balance and appeal. If you have a lot of pictures, art, and other articles placed around your home and you want to shorten your dusting time, you need to sit down and think about which articles you can live without. I guess your choice comes down to whether you value speed of cleaning or possession of objects.

As I looked around the bedroom, I saw that the windows and mirrors were shiny. The furniture was dusted. The bed neatly made, and no clothing or anything else lay around on the chairs and bed. I thought, *This was done by a bachelor. A lot of women wouldn't believe it!*

Lesson Learned

If you don't do your work in the correct order, you will be doing some of the jobs more than once, and it will take more time.

Where to now? I thought. *Well, the bathroom is right here, and it is a logical choice if I am going to work my way out of this end of the house and toward the end zone, which is the kitchen.*

Chapter 2

THE MASTER BATHROOM

As I stood in the bathroom doorway and looked at my next project, I thought, *I am sure that this is a task that everyone hates. People usually don't like to clean up after themselves or have the time after they perform their personal tasks, such as shaving or cutting the hair out of their noses.*

Suddenly a thought from the past jumped into my mind. I realized something I learned in OCS was really going to pay off for me here.

When I went to OCS right after I graduated from college, my first cleaning station was the head. For non-navy people, the head, known in the army as the latrine, is the bathroom for the sailors. It consists of a large room with about ten to fifteen showers, the same number of sinks, and the same number of heads, which are called toilets in civilian terms. The boys' or girls' locker room in high school or college is probably similar. The two most unpleasant objects to clean are the heads (toilet) and the showers. I got stuck with both of them!

Back then we were made to use the old reliable Dutch cleanser with the silly little Dutch girl in her silly wooden clogs and silly white bonnet on the label. We also had scrub brushes, toothbrushes, and towels. My mission was to make sure that all the scum between the tiles in the shower floor was gone so when the inspector rubbed his finger down the grout line, it didn't have any soap scum in it. The toilets had to shine. What made it really important to me was that if I didn't do a good job, then I would get a red gig, and when you got five red gigs, you had to march an hour on the weekend before you could go on liberty. Since I was a liberty hound, I had to make sure that my showers and shitters sparkled like diamonds so I could be one of the first OCS candidates out of the gate! Thinking back, if I had to do it over again, I would put ribbons on the toilet seats and place a rose on each toilet tank. That probably would have gotten a good rise out of the inspector.

Where to Start

So much for daydreaming, Sid. Back to the job, I thought.

Before I began my task, I stopped to evaluate what I had done over and over again in the bedroom because I didn't do the jobs in the right sequence. I surely didn't want to redo my work three times again.

As I thought about the tasks ahead, I realized that I had to clean the shower, sink, counter, mirror, tub, floor, and toilet. *What order should I attack them?* My brain whispered, *I should begin with the task that is farthest from the door and work to the exit.* I discovered later that it is best to work clockwise around the room from the exit door.

But wait a minute! I remembered that the bathroom usually has dust, hair, and other things on the floor. Plus there are also toothbrushes, toothpaste, and shaving gear in the way. I thought of the mess I made one time in trying to wash the floor without sweeping first. I need to prepare the room first. *So why not dust everything and then clean up the floor before getting anything wet?*

I found an old towel and started dusting the highest places. Yep, I remembered that dust falls, so I started at the windows and top of the shower enclosure and worked myself downward. Next I moved to the counter around the raised bathtub and the counter around the sink.

What I could not pick up with the rag I brushed onto the floor. Then I took a broom and swept it up into a pile and then tried to sweep it into a dustpan. The problem was that there was still debris in the grout spaces between the tiles and also in the corners that I could not get with a broom and dustpan.

"What about a dust buster?" I got my trusty dust buster and started sucking the dust balls, hair, and sand up. The only problem was that the exhaust from the dust buster blew everything everywhere before I could get it sucked up. Then I thought of my vacuum cleaner with the hose attachment. It can suck the debris up, and I can get into the corners and other areas where the sweeper will not go. As the vacuum inhaled the dust and debris from the floor, I thanked whoever invented the vacuum cleaner because it worked perfectly, and in a short time I had the bathroom completely dust-free and ready to clean.

Now the big decision was where to start. The john and the shower are both at the far end of the bathroom next to each other. I chose the toilet.

Trivia Time-Out

Now, I don't know if you are a trivia expert or not, but I do know that if you go to cocktail parties or out to dinner with friends, there are times when a lull in the conversation occurs. If this happens, you might find the following information helpful as a conversation continuer. Contrary to what most people think, Thomas Crapper was not the inventor of the flush toilet. Sir John Harrington, a British nobleman and godson of Queen Elizabeth I, was credited with inventing and installing the first flush toilet around 1596. I haven't been able to find out if that's why he was knighted.

It wasn't until the 1780s that Mr. Crapper came along and perfected the flush toilet. He was a plumber and had several inventions. The one I like best is the ballcock. Beats me what it is, but I like the name. Even though he didn't invent the flush toilet, it is possible that he had a better marketing plan because he received most of the credit. Now you know why some people refer to the toilet as "the john" or the "crapper." All of that happened in the modern day, however, and supposedly King Minos of Crete had the first flushing toilet recorded in history, and that was more than 2,800 years ago. If you want to know more, go check it out on the Internet!

Back to the task at hand! First I poured a solution of VDW into the bowl, scrubbed the bowl and underneath the lip around it with the toilet brush, and then flushed it down. VDW is a solution made up of one cup of vinegar and a squirt of Dawn dishwashing liquid in a gallon of water. From now on it will be known as VDW, and it can be used in a spray bottle or in a mop bucket.

Then I sprayed the outside of the john with VDW, and with a rag I wiped off the top of the tank, cleaned behind the lid, lifted the lid, and wiped the underside of the lid, the seat, including the bottom side of it, the lip of the toilet, the base, and the floor behind it. Then I took a towel and dried everything off, making a special effort to dry the handle and any other metal objects on the john. Yes, I saved the bowl for last so as not to dirty the rest of the toilet.

I had learned the hard way from a previous house cleaner who didn't do a very good job that if the metal parts aren't dried carefully, especially if commercial cleaners had been used, the cleaner corrodes the metal, and you are left with pitted toilet fixtures. When I confronted her about the problem, she simply said, "Oh, it happens everywhere." There's no telling how many bathrooms she has screwed up. Some people use laundry soap, and I usually use VDW. Either one is a good way to avoid the corroding problem and does just as good a job.

When I finished I stood up and looked at my masterpiece. *A spit-shined toilet*, figurative speaking of course. Thank you, OCS training!

Here's a tip: A secret to keeping the john clean is to keep a toilet bowl brush in a holder right next to the toilet for a quick fix. I guess you could equate it with brushing your teeth. Brush your teeth to eliminate bad breath. Brush out your bowl when it needs it, and your bowl doesn't have bad breath.

The Shower

Trivia Time-Out

The first showers were actually waterfalls, usually cold but efficient. Next came pouring water over your head from a large jug. The Egyptians got fancy and had private rooms in their homes where their servants bathed them.

The Greeks were the first people to have showers. Maybe that's where the joking comment "Be careful when you bend over to pick up the soap" came from. Then the Romans came up with their bathhouses, an idea that spread throughout the Mediterranean.

In about 1860 the French supposedly built the first modern shower. It was a communal shower for the French Army and used as an economic hygiene measure. Gotta kill those crabs!

The shower is a place that can really get grungy if it isn't tended to on a regular basis. When most people finish showering, they turn off the water, grab a towel, dry off, and step out of the shower without doing any cleanup work.

Most showers are all tile—tile plus glass or fiberglass. Mine happens to be a six-by-six one with tile, a fair amount of glass, and a glass door. It's not big enough for a cocktail party but plenty of room to move around while one is taking a shower. Yes, it is more area to clean, but I don't have to leave the door open when I bend over to pick up soap or to squeegee the stall after I finish my shower.

Consider the following tip: The biggest tip I can recommend is to go to a commercial cleaning store and purchase a large squeegee of about fourteen inches wide and use it on the glass and even the tile after you finish showering. Once you master this, you will have a cleaner shower for a longer time, which means easier and less cleaning jobs.

I also learned to dry off completely, especially your feet, before I would get out of the shower. By drying your feet, you don't need a bath mat that you have to pick up after you finish, and you don't get the floor wet. You also avoid the task of drying the floor when finished. These habits may take a while to acquire, but when you do them, you will take less time to clean up after a shower.

Since I vacuumed the floor of the shower when I vacuumed the bathroom floor, there won't be any hair or other debris to clean up. As I step into the shower to begin my task, I look to see if anything is growing on the walls or in the corners. If so, a little Clorox and a small brush will take care of it.

However, if you are growing a penicillin farm—I mean mold in your shower—you are in for a big loss of yardage. Instead of punting, the best play is to fill a spray bottle with Clorox made with one cup of Clorox and three cups of water. Spray the mold well, get out of the bathroom, and take a time-out on the sideline! Oh, yes, don't forget to turn the exhaust fan on before you leave. When you return to the playing field, there might some patches that need to be spot-sprayed and scrubbed with a brush or toothbrush.

Once the mold is gone, I spray the tile with either VDW or a commercial tile cleaner, and using a rag and or scrub brush, I wash away the soap and scum. I also remember to clean the soap dish on the wall and the windowsill. They're easy things to miss. Just remember that most commercial sprays are toxic and can pit the metal fixtures, so be sure to dry them well before you finish, preventing pitting.

After the soap scum and scale are scrubbed away from the tile and grout, I take a pan from the kitchen, fill it with water from the showerhead, and throw it against the wall to rinse off the tile. You guessed it. I got pretty wet, so on future plays I stripped to my birthday suit and rinsed away. Finally I got wise and attached one of those handheld shower sprayers and sprayed away!

If the shower tile doesn't really shine, I rinse it down again with vinegar and water. I am guessing that the vinegar rinse cuts any more soap scum left on the tile. One house cleaner I know still uses the old-fashioned Comet and then washes it down with dishwashing soap. It also seems to work very well.

With the tile done, I turn to the glass walls and door and spray them with the VDW and wash them with either a rag or large brush. You guessed it! I then run my bare hand over the glass to feel any spots that I might have missed.

If your VDW solution is overly strong, meaning that it has too much soap, it might leave a streak on the glass. But if you use a squeegee, the window ends up dry and really clear. Be sure and take old newspaper or a paper towel to dry the spots around the edge.

As I step out of the shower and say to myself, "Great job." The tile is clean. The glass is clean, and the floor is clean. I bet I would even have gotten a blue gig when I was in OCS. In case you are wondering, red gigs are for screw ups, and blue gigs negate red gigs and are awarded for doing an outstanding job. (They are kind of similar to the "get out of jail free" cards in Monopoly.)

What next? I ponder. Right next to the shower is the bathtub.

Trivia Time-Out

I thought back to when I was a kid in a family of five. Like other families in the late '40s and early '50s, all we had was one bathroom with only a tub and no shower. This was for my mom, dad, two sisters, and me. How did we ever live with only one bathroom? I can remember more than once when one of us desperately needed to use the john and someone else was in there. It seems like my baby sister Sally was always banging on the door and frantically yelling, "I need to go to the bathroom! It's an emergency!" while one of us was using it, usually sister Susie doing her hair or whatever young girls did in the bathroom. Living alone I don't have that problem.

Back to the Game

The tub in my master bathroom is really a Jacuzzi that I rarely use anymore, so cleaning it is a piece of cake. Since I wiped it down earlier when I was cleaning up all the dust, etc., all I have to do is spray it down with 409 or VDW and wipe it dry.

However, when I did use it on a regular basis, I rinsed it as the water went down, and then wiped it dry with a towel to get rid of the body oil. Because of that, I was able to get away with spraying it with VDW and wiping it out. Plastic and fiberglass have to be kept clean so that you can avoid using anything that will scratch the finish. The new cleaners are easy to spray on, leave for a few minutes, scrub with a rag or brush, and then wipe down to get anything that didn't dissolve. As I mentioned before, be careful to wipe off the metal fixtures so the chemical doesn't mar them. To be environmentally safe and avoid the toxins, I suggest the VDW solution. Some spots may need a little elbow grease, or you can use one of those Soft Scrub products and then wash the Jacuzzi down. A good rinsing finishes off the task.

Joke Time-Out

A lawyer was trying a murder case for a man named Wright. When the jury went out to make their decision during a hot summer, he went home to take a bath and cool off while the jury was deliberating. He was just finishing his bath and was cleaning the tub when the phone rang. The wife took the message and went to the bathroom to give him the message. She opened the bathroom door, and there he was bent over the tub in his birthday suit, washing suds down the drain. Not thinking about the situation in front of her, she said, "They aren't hanging Wright."

He stood up, looked at his wife, and said with a disgusting look, "Nag, nag, nag."

At one time I lived with a girlfriend in Atlanta. I remember how proud she was the first time she cleaned the bathroom. It looked really nice and clean. The first time I stepped into the bathtub to take a shower, I noticed how shiny and clean the bottom of the tub was. She cleaned the bottom of the tub; however, she neglected to clean the sides. I didn't score any brownie points when I pointed it out to her.

Back to the game

The bathroom sink and counter is another job that can be very difficult if you are the person who doesn't clean up after yourself and leaves everything willy-nilly. If that's the case, you have to clean up and put things away before you can tackle the real job.

To make things simple and easy to clean, all I leave on the counter is a bottle of hand soap and a small towel to dry my hands. Everything else goes in the medicine cabinet or the cabinet below the sink. Before I lay the bottle of hand soap aside, I run water over it and wash it off. It seems that no matter how neat I am, the soap always seeps around the outside of the bottle. With the sink clear of objects, it is time to begin.

Because I have learned from the past, I start high and finish low and spray the mirror with VDW, rub it with a damp cloth, go over it again with my hand to feel any minute spots, and then squeegee and wipe off the remaining drops This is a lot easier to do if I remember to wipe off the food particles that tend to flip on the mirror when I floss. With the mirror cleaned, I start on the sink below it.

If it is overly dirty, I start with Soft Scrub because it is so easy to work with and does such a good job. Since there aren't a lot of spots and smears to clean up, the job goes well, and I use the VDW. A small sponge or cloth works fine. I make sure to get all metal faucets and drains rinsed and dried off in order to not leave any stains or liquids that will pit the metal.

I need to say one thing before I go any further. I want to tell you how my father's shaving routine influenced my sisters' and my cleanup of the sink. Our dad was one of the biggest neat freaks I have ever met. I can remember watching him shave in the morning.

First he would fill the sink with hot running water. Then he would apply pink Life Boy soap to his washcloth and wash his face and then rinse it with the cloth as if he was preparing himself for surgery. The next step was to shake the can of shaving cream with the menthol smell and carefully apply it to his whiskers. Then came the big shave that every little boy envies as his daddy carefully shaves all the stubble off his face without cutting himself or slitting his own throat. The shaving finale begins as he wipes off his face with his washrag, splashes a little water on it, and gently dries his freshly shaved face with the white towel. The crowning event comes as he gently pours out a small amount of that Mennen skin bracer into his hands and slaps it on his face. I can still remember the commercial. SLAP! Slap! "Thanks, I needed that!" You probably have to be an old geezer to remember that ad.

Cleanup was an important part that my sisters and I marveled at. First he dried and put his razor and shaving cream back in the cabinet. Then as the water ran out of the sink, he took the washcloth and carefully made sure that all the shaving cream, soap, etc. went down the drain so there was no ring around the sink. Finally he took a towel and gently dried the sink and entire counter so it looked like no one had actually used it. To me, Dad's ritual was like a coach drawing a play on a chalkboard while I sat in rapt attention.

The reason I mention this is that later in life when I was visiting my baby sister Sally and I shaved in her bathroom, she came in after me to use the sink and yelled, "Wait a minute. Get back here and dry the sink like Daddy did!" That is an experience I still remember and think about sometimes as I am drying the sink after I shave or brush my teeth.

The Floor

As I look at the floor, I realize that I'm going to need a bucket of VDW, mop, small scrub brush, and cloth. What am I going to do? I can carry in the water in a bucket filled in the kitchen, but with my luck I will probably spill it somewhere along the way. Or I can fill it in the tub or shower, but then I will mess them up again. Then I look over at the toilet, and another idea hits me. *I have just cleaned the toilet, and it's conveniently right here.* Even if I spill a little water around it, no big deal! I pour a cup of vinegar and a little Dawn into the toilet bowl, making VDW. Then I drop my cleaning rag into the toilet, wring it out, and scrub the floor on my hands and knees. I rinse out the rag a couple of times as I wash the floor. When I rinse the rag out in the toilet bowl, I can see any debris I pick from the floor. When I finish, I rinse out the rag one more time and flush the somewhat dirty water down the toilet, dry off the toilet bowl, and then dry the floor as I back out of the bathroom.

I had an amusing talk with my editor about the shower section. Back when I first cleaned the shower, I mentioned that I got wet when I tossed the water against the wall with the pan from the kitchen. I said that I had stripped down to my birthday suit but never mentioned anything about putting my clothes back on. She thought that I continued cleaning the tub in my birthday suit then was on my hands and knees scrubbing the floor. It is pretty funny when you think about it, but I am never going to let you know!

Using a squeegee after you use the shower
makes more time between cleanings.

Not bad! I think as I take one last look at my finished masterpiece. The toilet sparkles. The shower and Jacuzzi shine, and the mirror and sink give off a bright radiance.

Lesson Learned

Always be ready to think outside of the box. By doing this, I figured out a better way to rinse the shower and to utilize the clean toilet as a bucket. Both made the job easier and saved time.

Before I began the next room, the living room, I realize that I had been working by the seat of my pants and didn't have a game plan. If

I didn't get organized, I was going to be fumbling my way through the rest of the house, and it would take twice as long it should. As a result, I declared this halftime so that I could go to my locker room to regroup and plan for the second half.

Chapter 3

HALFTIME

In the locker room I review my plays—the good ones, the bad ones, and the ones I did out of sequence, which caused me to do some work twice. This next half, instead of a "seat of the pants" game plan, I'm going to have a real game plan.

Each of the cleaning sequences is a series of plays in the game similar to kickoff, offense, defense, punt, goal-line stand, etc. Every series will be run in a clockwise direction around the room so I can remember where I am if I get distracted. I will always do them in the same order in an effort to not mess up work that I have already completed.

1. **Scout the job out.**

    I found that it is beneficial to scout out the whole job before I start. Then I take a look at each room before I plunge into them.

2. **Pick up what is lying around and put it in its place or throw it away.**

    Here again it is a good idea to pick up all rooms before you begin the actual work so you don't have to stop and pick up things as you go along. It is your option.

3. **Dust.**

4. **Clean the glass, mirrors, and windows.**

5. **Vacuum and/or mop the floor.**

   There will be a lot of debate on where cleaning the floor fits in the series. Some say you should do it first, let the dust settle, dust, and continue the series. The trouble with vacuuming first is that you will probably have to go back and run the vacuum again to clean up your footprints and anything else you may have dropped when you were doing the other jobs. Put it where you want, but for this program it is series number five.

6. **Have a postgame wrap-up.**

   Before packing up and leaving, go back over all of the work you have done and see if you have overlooked anything. If so, correct it before you call it a complete game.

7. **Put away all of your cleaning gear, pop a cool one, and mark up another victory.**

The Playbook in the back of the book provides you with the complete gameplan laid out in detail explaining each series, what equipment is necessary to run the plays in the series, and the steps to successfully complete the series. Use it as your playbook and make necessary notes to go along with it.

Chapter 4

THE LIVING ROOM

Living rooms in general come in two styles—a formal one used only to entertain guests and the informal. Mine is informal. It's where we sit if someone comes to visit, where I watch television, where I read the newspaper, and where I sit when solving the problems of the world. To me it's my favorite room because it has two sets of sliding glass doors that allow for a panoramic view over a beautiful fifty-five-acre lake. The view enables me to enjoy many fabulous sunsets and reflections of the homes and other lights from across the lake at night. The other side of the living room has three double-hung seven-foot windows and a front door that allow for great cross ventilation when the wind is right. Maybe you are wondering what the cross ventilation has to do with cleaning my house. That comes later!

The ref blows the whistle, and the second half begins. I immediately go into my first series of plays.

Scouting

While scouting out the rest of the house, I site the following discrepancies:

- Living room—I look high and notice that the ceiling doesn't have any cobwebs, the fan has a little dust on it, and the AC registers look clean. The picture frames need dusting.

  As I look around the room the second time, I see a beer glass and coaster on the table beside the recliner along with reading glasses, a book, TV control, and a couple of books. There is a pair of shoes by the chair, newspapers scattered on the floor, and a pile of magazines lying on the coffee table. The glass sliding doors need cleaning, and the rest is normal cleanup.

- Dining room—I notice cobwebs on the light fixture. On the table there are some wine glasses, dessert dishes, silverware, and cloth napkins left over from dinner last night.
- Second bathroom—It's a mess! The toilet bowl has a ring in it. The sink looks like it hasn't been cleaned in a couple of months. The mirror has spots and remains from tooth-brushing and flossing splattered on it. The shower is growing penicillin. The towels are all dirty. The rug is shoved over in the corner, and the floor needs scrubbing. Outside of that, everything looks great.
- Second bedroom—It looks okay except for dusting the furniture and straightening up the bedspread because it is seldom used and the door is usually kept closed.
- Office—Ugh! First I spy a cobweb in the corner. As usual there are papers all over the desk. The wastebasket is full. Books are on the floor, and a jock strap is hanging from the floor lamp next to the door.
- Man Cave—The man cave is where men can be boys and get away with it. This room is no exception, and it is a mess.

- Kitchen—The kitchen looks like a minor hurricane has hit it. The sink is full of dishes. The counter to the left of the sink has mail, car keys, sunglasses, and other items I have left as I came into the house. The salt and pepper shakers and other spices are spread around the counter by the stove. There are a couple of pots on the stove, and the oven door is half open. I would say that it looks like a typical single man's kitchen.

Pickup

As I look at what I have to do before I start cleaning, I realize the extra work I have created by not picking up after myself. The thought runs through my mind, *If you had paid attention to what your mother said about putting things away and cleaning up after yourself, you wouldn't have all of this mess to clean up, and you could be enjoying yourself, playing tennis, or going to the beach.* Since I can't wave my hands in the air like a magician and make everything return to where it belongs and have the dishes jump into the dishwasher, I guess I had better get to work.

I begin in the living room and follow the same pattern as I did when I was scouting the place. I put the shoes away, sort the magazines into read and unread piles, place the unread stack on the sofa, and throw the others along with the newspaper into the trash. Reading glasses and other items on the side table are put in their places, and the beer glass and coaster are removed to the kitchen.

The dining room poses a little problem because the sink is already full of dishes, so I have to take the time to soak the dishes already in the sink, wash the dried food off them, and place into the dishwasher. Then I have to pick up the dirty dishes, silverware, and wine glasses from the dining room table and go through the same procedure with them.

In the meantime, I think of how much time I could have saved and how much easier and faster the job would be if I had cleaned the table last night. The food would not have been stuck on the plates like glue, and everything would be in the dishwasher and ready to be put away this morning.

Since then I have developed the Tom Sawyer play for handling this situation.

Tom Sawyer Play

Whenever you have guests over, whether one or many, get up and start clearing the table. Usually there will be one or two who will start helping. Instead of telling them to sit down and that you will get it tomorrow, let them help. The more you can get accomplished before everyone leaves the table, the less you will have to clean up after they are gone. After all, a single man needs all of the help he can get!

With the dining room picked up, I go to the office and stack the papers into two neat piles, pick up the books, return them to their shelves, and remove my special decoration, the jock strap, and put it into the dirty laundry basket.

There isn't much I can do in the second bathroom except put the toothpaste and toothbrush away and put the dirty washcloth and towel in the laundry.

In the kitchen I put the salt and pepper shakers and spices away, take the mail to the office, and place the pots and pans in the sink for them to soak in baking soda, dish soap, and water. Unfortunately they will have to be washed when I clean the kitchen.

Now that I have scouted and picked up articles that are out of place and threw them out or put them in their places, I am ready to do the rest of the house room by room and complete all series as I go along.

Dusting

First I bring in the ladder and clean the ceiling fan in the living room. I could use the fan blade brush with an extension, but I don't because I bent one of the blades using it once and had to replace all of them. All I can say is be careful when you are cleaning the fan blades.

Since I only have one more use for the ladder, I clean the light fixture over the dining room table, remove the ladder, and get underway with the rest

Trivia Time–Out

Microfiber was first developed in the 1950s but wasn't perfected until Japanese Drs. Okamoto and Hikota started working on it in the 1960s and came up with many industrial applications. Ultra Suede was one of the first. In 2007, Rubbermaid was the first major company in the United States to develop microfiber products.

The microfiber thread can be as thin as a hundredth the size of a human hair. It is water repellent, but if it is split, it then becomes absorbent. The shapes, sizes, and combinations of synthetic fibers are selected for specific characteristics, including softness, toughness, absorption, water repellency, electrodynamics, and filtering capabilities.

Athletic wear is made of microfiber because of its wicking ability, which keeps the wearer cooler. In the 2006–07 National Basketball Association season, better known as the NBA, they experimented with basketballs made from microfiber but rejected the idea because the athletes said the ball bounced differently and left cuts on their hands. What a bunch of wimps!

For more information, google "microfiber" to explore more about this material.

Back to the Game

With everything on the ceiling cleaned, my first trip around the room—always in a clockwise movement—I check out the mirrors, pictures, and anything else hanging on the wall and dust what needs to be done. The next circuit I do all of the furniture along the walls. First I do the lamp shades on the end tables at each end of the sofa. If they are smooth, I can dust them off with a microfiber rag. If they are pleated or rough, I use the brush on the end of the vacuum hose. In being thorough, I don't forget the lightbulb and parts of the lamp covered by the shade and of course the base of the lamps. The bulb and parts covered by the shade are easy places to forget. With the higher dusting done, I move to the furniture.

As I dust the glass tops of the end tables, I notice that they have a few smudges, but I dust them anyway and will come back later and wash them. Washing them is a lot easier if the dust has been removed.

I also remember to get the legs of the tables and the back side of the lower shelf, being mindful to pick up any artistic decorations or other objects and dust under them. If the furniture is bamboo or some other rough or carved surface, sometimes I will use the vacuum hose with the brush on the end to get into the crevices.

The more I use the vacuum hose and brush, the more places I find that it does a better job and makes my job easier and quicker. Dusting something like a bookcase or sound equipment are great examples because the brush can get into areas that a rag won't reach like the top of books and around the knobs on the sound equipment.

Something else often overlooked is the flat-screen TV. It usually comes with a cleaning cloth and instructions to use only water. If you lose the cloth, replace it with a soft lint free cloth or microfiber cloth. Remember that some microfiber cloths are made to be abrasive, so make sure you know what kind you are using.

After I complete dusting the furniture against the walls, I attack any furniture standing in the middle of the room. Most living rooms have a coffee table in front of the sofa and usually a chair at each end of the table to form a conversation area.

To me the two most important tables in the home are the coffee table and dining room table because people sit around them and are able to notice any flaws or discrepancies. For that reason I take special care to make sure that they are immaculate and neatly decorated.

The base of my coffee table is two green dolphins frolicking in the water and the top is clear glass. To dust the dolphins, I use a long-hair brush and then go over it with the vacuum hose and brush to remove all the dust and particles. Then I make sure the glass is spotless on the top and the bottom side. Over time glass can get a film on it and become somewhat clouded. It happens so slowly that often we never notice it.

Trivia Question

Do you know what the most overlooked item is when it comes to dusting? It's the fabric on the furniture. The chair and sofa set just sit there while we dust the wood and usually neglect to vacuum the fabric.

I found out about the fabric when I happened to pull the vacuum hose with attachment over my white sofa. The path it left was snow white, and the rest of the sofa looked light gray in comparison. After I vacuumed the entire sofa and returned it to a whiter white, I made sure to include vacuuming the fabric on the furniture once in a while.

Cleaning the Glass and Mirrors

Now it is glass time in the living room. Working clockwise, I start with the windows by the front door. There are three double-hung windows with twelve panes in each section. It is really pretty easy to do with a bottle of VDW, a soft brush to scrub, a squeegee, and some newspapers to dry with. I just spray the top six in each section at a time, scrub them with a brush, squeegee the six, wipe the edges of the glass to remove any other water on the pane, and then do the six panes below. I also dry off the sill and any other place water may have dropped.

Next are the glass tops on the end tables by the sofa. I remove any small items that might be on the table and place them on the sofa. Then I pick up the lamp, spray the glass top, scrub it down, and squeegee or dry it with a rag. After I replace the lamp, I wipe off any excess water on the tabletop, and replace the objects back to their original places. With some lamps being quite heavy, you may have to clean half of the glass, move the lamp to the clean part, clean the other half, and place everything back where it belongs.

Pick up. Don't dust around anything.

Since the coffee table is right in front of me and the only other glass in the room except for the sliding glass doors, I do it next. As I mentioned, the coffee table and dining room table are the two most scrutinized objects in the house. After I wash it down with VDW and a brush, I run my hand over it to feel any spots that I can't see and then squeegee and dry up any extra water with old newspaper or a microfiber cloth.

With that done, I then look at the top of glass from an angle to see if there are any streaks or places I missed. I also look for any fingerprints or other blemishes on the underside of the tabletop and take care of them. Sometimes it is necessary to clean one side and then flip it over and clean the other side if it develops a film or streaks on it. I usually leave the top flipped, but some tables require flipping them back to their original position.

Now I finish the room by doing the sliding glass doors. Before I begin work on the doors, I make sure I vacuum the tracks and remove any debris in them. If they stick a little, I sometimes slide a bar of soap along the rails. You can also spray WD-40 or silicone on the rails so they move easier.

First it may be necessary to wipe the window with a damp cloth to remove the insects that thought that they were kamikaze pilots.

Next I apply the VDW and wash the window. Since the windows are large you can either continue to use the spray bottle or wash it with a large rag or brush from a bucket of VDW. Here I particularly like to run my hand over the glass to see if I can feel any spots that I may have missed.

Finally I squeegee and then wipe off excess water from the window and give it a close final inspection by looking at the windows from an angle to catch any flaws during the process.

How to Squeegee

When you squeegee anything, you should always dry the blade dry before every stroke. You can pull from top to bottom or crossways across the glass. Before you begin, dry a two-inch strip across the beginning and always start on a dry spot to get the best results.

Before the beginning of each stroke, dry the blade and overlap the previous stroke by about three inches to eliminate streaks from water left on the glass.

When you have completed the last stroke go back and dry with a rag or squeegee any water left on the glass. With a little practice you should become a real pro.

When I'm cleaning the outside of the windows, I choose one of the following: either I repeat the play from inside or clean them when I wash down the porch with the hose.

When I use the hose, I wash down everything and then wash the windows with VDW. After I hose them clean, I squeegee and then wipe the remaining water spots with a microfiber cloth or old newspaper.

The Floor

Carpeting

A friend a few houses away has a Golden Retriever. When I asked him how he cleans up all the dog hair, he responded, "On a windy day we just open the sliders on one side of the house and the windows and doors on the other. After the wind blows for a while all the hair ends up against the wall on the other side of the house. All we have to do then is go over and vacuum it up. It saves a lot of time!" That's thinking outside of the box.

Since this is the last play in the series for the living room, I sometimes prefer to complete all of the earlier plays in all rooms and then vacuum the whole house at one time. When I do this, I start from the room in the back part of the house and work myself in a backward direction to my exit. By backing out I am like an Indian covering his tracks so that those trailing him can't find his trail.

In doing a single room, I use the same principle of starting in the farthest corner of the room and work backward to the exit point. In doing this, I know where I start each time and also don't have to step on the freshly vacuumed carpet.

Some carpets are plush, and the vacuum leaves marks where it has gone. In this case it is important to vacuum in some kind of pattern so that when you are finished, it looks neat and not like someone has vacuumed in which every direction. If you have an artistic flare, you can even vacuum a pattern in the carpet just like they do at professional football fields.

Although this is the final play of the floor series for the living room and time to move on to the dining room, we need to talk about tile and other types of floors.

Tile

Several years ago because my allergies were bugging me and to "keep up with the Joneses," I decided to get my whole house tiled. Now when I do something, I don't do it halfway. I had all of the carpet in the house removed and replaced with eighteen-inch square tile. That meant no carpeting anywhere and only a couple of rugs by the beds, in the baths, and at the front and back door. From the beginning it was an adventure and continues to be a learning experience every day.

Trivia Time-Out

I picked a German tile company recommended by one of the builders for which I had done landscaping. The workers started by moving all of my furniture to the garage and proceeded to rip up all of the carpeting in my house. I lived in one side of the house as they worked on the rest.

First they did the living room by finding the center of the room and worked outward toward the walls. They were very professional and laid out the lines with a laser and proceeded to lay the tile. Everything went smoothly. Then something interesting happened along the way.

I don't remember exactly how it all started. They were working and speaking in German. Suddenly one of them let out a swear word in English. One of the other Germans asked me what it meant. I explained. One of them said the word again, and we all laughed. Then another swear word was spoken. We went through the same routine, and it became funnier and funnier. Before long I realized I was becoming a profane language teacher. We were like a bunch of seven-year-old kids laughing at ourselves and at what was happening.

At the end of work on the second day, after they laid the living room, I happened to drop a screwdriver on one of the tiles. It sounded hollow. I dropped it again on several more tiles and realized that a lot of the tiles had hollow spaces under them because they hadn't spread the adhesive evenly. I marked about thirty tiles, all of which they removed and replaced. Everything went smoothly for the rest of the house.

About a year later I accidently dropped a quarter on the floor in the master bedroom and found several other tiles with the same problem. When my bookkeeper was working one day, I mentioned the problem to her. She said, "Oh, don't worry about it. I have several tiles in my house with the same problem. I just call them my singing tiles." I took her advice and let it slide and have yet to have a tile crack. They are a lot stronger than I ever guessed. Years later, none have ever cracked.

Back to the Game

When it came to cleaning the tile, I knew that it had to be vacuumed before I mopped it. Since I had my Hoover WINDTUNNEL upright, I started using it. The attached vacuum hose with the different attachments came in handy as well.

When I was visiting a vacuum store to pick up parts for my sweeper, the salesman said that on tile it is best to disconnect the beater bar on the bottom of the sweeper because all it does is blow the dust away instead of picking it up. I tried it on mine but can't tell if it makes any difference or not.

After a couple months of pushing the upright sweeper around, I decided that a tank-type vacuum with hose might work better. Instead of purchasing a new one, I remembered my shop vac in the garage and gave it a try.

Lo and behold, I found it to be fantastic. It may be a little noisier; however, the suction is unbelievable, and it will suck some pretty sizable objects from about four inches away with no problem. I have sucked up a couple of socks, but they either get caught in beginning of the hose or against the baffle inside the tank, so it doesn't ruin the machine.

After I used the shop vac a couple of times, I decided that the width of the attachment was narrower than I would like, so I went to a vacuum repair shop and purchased a wider residential attachment with better brushes. I now have the best of both worlds—the suction of a shop vac and a wider residential attachment.

Advantages of a Shop Vac

First of all, don't get a real big shop vac but get one with good suction. Six gallons is more than adequate. If the attachment isn't wide enough for you or doesn't have any brushes on it, go to a vacuum repair shop and get a wide one with brushes. You will probably need an adapter to reduce the size to fit the attachment. It really does a great job.

The advantages include the following:

1. It has very good suction, and you can pick up debris from up to four inches from the intake.
2. You can pick up bigger things that a regular vacuum can't and not screw it up because the hose is larger and everything falls into the holding tank.
3. Besides the inside of the house, it works great around a pool deck and front door and is a lot better than sweeping or blowing with a leaf blower. It also doesn't care what it picks up, and the sucked-up lizards get a real joy ride.
4. You can use it to suck up water. It is better if you empty the trash from the tank first so you don't end up with a wet mess.
5. It is made of plastic and light for the size, and it also has bigger wheels, so it rolls easily.
6. It is easy to clean. I used to take the filter off and bang it against the inside of the garbage can. I found it is more fun to just take the top off the tank, lay it on the ground with the filter intact and use the leaf blower on it. Just don't get downwind from it. You can also take the hose and put in the discharge side of the vacuum and blow it clean.

7. You can switch the hose to the exhaust port and use it as a blower to clean your front porch or driveway if you have a long enough extension cord.

The shop vac can be a powerful and useful tool.

When it came to mopping the tile, I took into account what I saw the sailors do when swabbing the deck in the navy. I went to Home Depot and purchased a big "swabbie" mop, a bucket on wheels, and a wringer that hung on the side of the bucket. In order to save money, I purchased a plastic bucket instead of the heavier metal one. Penalty— fifteen yards for thinking cheaply! The first time I used it and went to squeeze the mop with the squeezer on the side of the bucket, the bucket fell over and spilled water all over the floor. A swabbie sailor I ain't!

After I tried several other ideas I called my Cuban friend Andy who sold cleaning supplies. I remember his instructions well, "You need a Cuban rag mop," he said.

"What the heck is a Cuban rag mop?" I queried.

He explained it, but I couldn't really grasp the idea. Then he told me to go down to the Cuban grocery and ask them for a Cuban rag mop.

I walked into the grocery and said, "I want a Cuban rag mop."

The salesman turned on his heels and quickly headed down the aisle behind him. I followed in hot pursuit. He took a quick right but didn't lose me. At the end of the next aisle was a pile of sticks. The first one he picked up was a three-quarters-inch dowel about four feet long with a male thread on the end of it. Then he picked up another dowel that was about eighteen inches long and about an inch and a half in diameter with a female thread drilled into it the middle of it. He screwed the long dowel into the shorter one and formed a T. Then picked up a chamois, handed them to me, and said, "Here's your Cuban rag mop. That will be $7.42."

I took the Cuban Rag mop home and ran some water in the kitchen sink, added some vinegar, soaked the chamois, wrung it out, and laid it on the floor. Then I placed the T on the chamois, folded it once, and started pushing back and forth. "Wow!" I exclaimed.

The Cuban rag mop is the easiest and best mop that I have ever used. It covers a good size area and is simple to use, rinse, and wring out. If I encounter a spot that is difficult to remove, I can apply enough pressure to wipe it clean. If the spot is really stubborn I can take my foot and really put pressure on the rag. Since it is so thin, the rag mop easily goes under most furniture in the house and is easy to store. What a deal!

Instead of the chamois, I have found that half of an old bath towel works better because it has more surface area and can pick up more dirt. When I am finished, all I have to do is to wring it out and throw it in the washer.

Cuban Rag Mop

Do you remember the old song "Rag Mop" from back, in the 50s? It goes, "Rag mop! R-A-G-G M-O-P-P, rag mop!" Google it and you can see several versions. The Ames Brothers version is the original. It is kind of corny but worth a look.

Mopping Procedure

Mopping is pretty easy. First I prepare the water for whatever part of the house I am going to mop. The source may be a bucket, the toilet, or a sink. With the Cuban rag mop I don't need a large amount of water and can tell when the water gets dirty. That is the time to change it. The formula for the water is normally one cup of vinegar per one gallon of water. Sometimes I add more vinegar and a larger squirt of Dawn. Be careful with the amount of soap because they say too much tends to stick to the tile and grout.

Then I begin in the farthest point and work backward to the water source so I don't walk over what I have mopped. I always remember the Indian covering his tracks.

There are other types of floors, and they will be covered in the playbook at the back of this book.

Lesson Learned

Think outside of the box, and you will find other ways of doing jobs.

Chapter 5

THE DINING ROOM

The dining room in comparison to the other rooms in the house should be a pretty easy room to clean. Size and decorations are probably the only determining factors on the time it takes to clean. Imagine having to clean the great halls back in the Middle Ages where they had a long table with benches along each side. They likely had the walls decorated with weapons of war like swords, shields, and tapestries. I can just imagine old people in brown robes working away with primitive brooms with torches on the wall as their only sources of light.

Today the dining room might be large or may only consist of a room with a buffet, a table, and four chairs. There are lots of sizes in between; however, you still get down to the basics, and the game plan will work in any situation.

I have already scouted out the room and cleaned up the plates and glasses from the table and dusted the lamp fixture above the table, but I still take a second look around and see what else needs to be done. Yep, I forgot the place mats and salt and pepper shakers.

With everything picked up, I can begin my dusting clockwise around the room, dusting the pictures on the walls, the mirror over the buffet, the statues on the buffet, and finally the top of the buffet and the table.

Since the tabletop is glass, I dust it to clean any debris on its top. Then I pull out all of the chairs, dusting their legs as I go, and then I do the legs of the tables. Since I will be vacuuming later, I leave them away from the table so I can run the vacuum under the table. I will wash the top on the next route when I do the glass and mirrors.

The mirror above the buffet is clean, so I can bypass it. If it did need cleaning, I would either lay something on the buffet top or wipe any spots off it after I washed the mirror.

The two big glass items are the table and large sliding doors, which allow a westward look out and across the lake where I see beautiful sunsets quite often. Both of these items are important because they are focal points.

Before I wash the sliding glass doors, I take the vacuum and suck up any debris in the sliders. Next I take a large sponge on a stick and wash down the glass doors and then run the palm of my hand over the glass to make sure I have it completely clean. The final step is using the squeegee to dry it. A squeegee is much faster and does a better job than trying to dry it with a cloth or towel. It also eliminates the chance of having lint stick on the window. After I wipe away any water droplets around the edge, I take a look at the glass from the sides to see if I can see any streaks and remove them if necessary.

The glass tabletop is just a large window laid flat and can be handled the same way as the sliding glass door. Use a spray bottle to apply the VDW and don't let the excess water drop off the glass and wet the carpet. Use a squeegee, towel, or old newspaper to dry.

Just remember, if you are having guests for dinner, they are going to be looking at the tabletop the whole meal. *Does that get your attention?*

Now I am down to the floor. Assuming that most dining rooms have carpet, the best place to start is underneath the table. If I didn't pull out all the chairs when I was dusting their legs, I do it now and run the vacuum. Then I carefully replace the chairs so it looks like a showroom floor under the table. Finally I have to select an exit door and then work backward from the other side of the dining room so I don't leave any footprints on the newly vacuumed carpet. That likely means vacuuming halfway around each side of the table to the exit.

With that completed, I am ready to move on to the extra bedrooms.

Chapter 6

THE OTHER BEDROOMS

These rooms can be really easy to clean or a complete fiasco depending on how often they are used or what they are used for. If they are used for storage and have all kinds of things stored in them, maybe it is easier to close the door and act like they aren't there.

If you are going to clean them, follow the playbook procedures of picking up, dusting, cleaning the glass and mirrors, and finally washing the floor. Close the door and move on.

Chapter 7

THE SECOND BATHROOM

Trivia Time-Out

Out of curiosity I looked at the definition of *bathroom* in Wikipedia and came up with the following: "A bathroom is a room for personal hygiene, generally containing a bathtub or shower and possibly a bidet." Lots of Americans don't even know what a bidet is. When I was younger, I had heard the word but never saw one until I was in the navy.

After OCS several of us neophyte ensigns (second lieutenants in all of the other armed forces) were flown to Naples, Italy, to meet our ships. We spent the first night there in a nice hotel, and each room had a bidet in the bathroom. I thought it was pretty neat and turned on the faucet full force and watched the stream of water as it squirted up about three feet. I laughed and went next door to see what my neighboring ensign was doing. When I knocked, he told me to come in, and I did. There I found him in the bathroom, sitting on the head (toilet) in his uniform. He had the bidet half full of water, and he was sitting there, carefully spit-shining his shoes. I broke out laughing and asked him if he knew what a bidet was. You guessed it. He didn't.

Back to the Game

I employ my game plan and scout the job out.

As I look into the second bathroom, I see cobwebs in the ceiling corners. The lamp fixture needs to be dusted, and one of the bulbs replaced. The mirror has toothpaste, floss splattering, smudges, and handprints on it. The counter has a can of shaving cream, a razor, an opened tube of toothpaste, and toothbrush spread out on it. The sink and faucets are all covered with soap scum. The shower hasn't been cleaned for quite some time and has soap scum on the tile and mold in the corners. The tub is in the same shape with footprints on the bottom of it. The head needs the dark ring around the bowl removed, and the underside of the seat needs cleaning. Finally the floor has dust balls, strings of hair, a loose piece of toilet paper, and the wastebasket is overflowing.

Cleaning up the sink involved placing the toothbrush and toothpaste back in the cabinet and picking up all of the items and dropping them into the wastebasket that I retrieved from the garage. Then I replaced the burnt-out bulb in the light fixture.

I clean the cobwebs in the corner, dust the lamp fixture, wipe off the counter, and I vacuum the bottom of the tub, the coping around the tub, and finish with the floor. Then I dust off the counter and vacuum the floor.

I clean the mirrors and the window in the shower with VDW or Windex equivalent. If that doesn't clean the window, you may have to use a bath and tile commercial spray to cut the soap scum and water spots. Sometimes straight vinegar will do the job.

With VDW, I clean the shower tile, shower door, bathtub, sink, counter, and finally the toilet bowl. Pour a cup of vinegar and squirt of Dawn in the bowl and wash the floor with the rag mop or an old towel. (If there are still water spots on the glass or tile, pour vinegar on a rag, wash the spots, let sit for a while, run your rag over them again, and then rinse and squeegee. They should disappear.)

If the tile and bathtub become overly soiled and the VDW won't cut it, I go to the following supplies and use them in the listed order as needed—first Soft Scrub and then bath and tub cleaner. (If I have mildew or mold, I mix up a potion of concentrated Clorox at the rate of one cup of Clorox to three cups of water.) Spray or wipe on the spot, wait five minutes, and everything should disappear. Rinse well.

Since the room is so small and I can use my rag mop and also get on my hands and knees to get behind the toilet, I pour some vinegar and a squirt of Dawn into the toilet and use it for my water source.

Trivia Time-Out

Unfortunately there isn't much history about the bathtub. I can tell you this, however: Millard Fillmore wasn't known for accomplishing much as president, but in 1850, he had the first bathtub installed in the White House. If nothing else, we can say he cleaned up the people in the White House.

It was in the year of 1883 that Kohler began producing cast-iron bathtubs in the United States. Before then I suppose they used those metal tubs that we saw in the movies. In 1928, Crane released the first colored bathtub in the United States.

In talking about the bathroom, I feel remiss in not telling you a short story about the toilet seat.

I remember when I was a little kid and finally tall enough to stand up to the toilet and pee like a man. At first my aim wasn't very good, and I managed to spray the seat, which won no points with my mother. I justified it as washing the seat. She didn't buy my reasoning.

I can also remember going on trips with my family. Dad would take me into the bathroom, and we would pee together. I remember more than once saying excitedly, "Let's make a cross, Daddy!" as we stood there.

After I finally learned and remembered the gentlemanly manners of lifting the seat, I did quite well for several years. That was until one night when I was home from college and had been out with the boys drinking beer.

I was in bed, and all was quiet until suddenly I heard a shriek from my mother. "Damn it, Sidney!" When she talked that way, I knew I was in trouble, but instead of getting up and facing her wrath, I pretended like I was sound asleep.

The next morning at breakfast it was rather quiet. Then my mom said, "You don't know what a cold and surprising shock it is to sit down on that cold toilet bowl when one is half asleep." She probably would have preferred to say, "To plant one's ass on that cold bowl." I was just happy that she was big enough that she didn't slip into the bowl or get stuck!

Later while I was in the navy, the toilet seat came up again. I stopped to visit a couple of young ladies I knew, and when I went in to use the head and picked up the seat, I saw written on the bottom side of the seat, "It's so nice to have a man around the house!"

In a conversation one night on the ship we got to talking about the subject and a salty navy chief explained how he straightened his son out. Above the toilet in a nice picture frame he wrote the following, "Be like dad, not like sis. Lift the seat before you piss!"

If I was a marriage counselor, I would have two solutions to the problem when a couple came in arguing about the toilet seat.

When couples argue about whether the seat should be up or down, there is another part of the toilet that they seem to forget about—the lid. Make it a rule that every time anyone, male or female, uses the toilet, they must close the lid when finished. In that way both have to open the lid, do their duty, and then close it. In that way, both go through the same motions when they complete their duties. There is no favoritism there. That's solution A.

As for solution B, consider this: I was in a friend's house and happened to see the master bathroom. There beside the toilet and the bidet was a urinal! How's that for equal rights?

With the floor done and the sink cleaned out, I am finished with the bathroom and ready for the next room.

Chapter 8

THE MAN CAVE

A book about single a man cleaning his house wouldn't be complete without a chapter on the man cave, so here it is. The following is taken from Wikipedia:

> A man cave is a male sanctuary, such as a specially equipped garage, spare bedroom, media room, den, or basement. It can be a spare bedroom inside the house, a media room, den or basement, garage, attic or office. It can also be outside the house such as a wooded shed or tool room, where guys can do as they please without fear of upsetting any female sensibility about house décor or design. Paula Aymer of Tufts University calls it the "last bastion of masculinity.
>
> While a wife may have substantial authority over a whole house in terms of design and decoration, she generally has no say about what gets "mounted on the walls" of a man's personal space. In other words, he is king!

I like that last statement!

Every man cave I have been in is very nicely kept, and the man king takes a lot of pride in it. As a result, it is neatly kept. I would say that it is a place where a man doesn't have to be told how to keep it clean. Nevertheless, the tips I have given in this book should make cleaning of your man cave quick and easy. Just follow the basic game plan. Remember, if you don't mess it up, it is easier to keep clean.

After I wrote the man cave part of this chapter, I realized that a single man doesn't have a master in his house unless he has a girlfriend who likes to play the master role. His house is his man cave.

Chapter 9

THE KITCHEN

Now we come to potentially the biggest mess in the whole house. If you tend to do any or all of the following, you can be in big trouble and may have a mountain of a task ahead of you. How does your kitchen look?

- When you cook, do you leave all the pots, pans, and utensils lying on the counter and even sometimes on the floor?
- When you are finished eating, do you simply place the dishes, knives, forks, and spoons in the sink?
- When you come in at night, do you unload everything you are carrying onto the kitchen counter and neglect to take them to the proper place in the house?

Let's assume the worst and that the kitchen is a mess!

If you have any of the above habits and you want to save time in keeping your house clean, you need to change your patterns.

Let's go back to the football field and assume that you are a tackle on the football team. At the beginning of each play you approach the line and get down into your three-point stance. When the center snaps the ball to the quarterback to begin the play, you stand up instead of just raising up slightly and staying in your blocking stance so you can block. As a result, you are in a vulnerable stance. The opposing lineman simply can run into you and knock you out of the way or worse yet, simply plow right over the top of you. So what you need to do is change your pattern of behavior and simply come up into your blocking stance rather than standing up straight. Then you will become a better blocker and not get knocked on your tail.

So what you need to do in the kitchen is change your patterns of behavior so that you don't make more work for yourself and make your job harder and longer. Here are five examples:

- When you come into the house, instead of unloading everything on the counter, take them to their ultimate locations—mail to the office, clothes to the closet or dirty clothes basket, and anything else back where it belongs.
- When you finish using spices, condiments, and other items in the kitchen, put them away instead of leaving them on the counter.
- After you use pots and pans and anything else the last time, wash them off and put them in the dishwasher or dry them and put them away in the pantry.
- Never leave anything on the kitchen counter that you aren't going to use right away. Put it away and get it later.
- When you are finished eating, rinse your plates and silverware and place them in the dishwasher and not in the sink.

If you can follow those five patterns of behavior, you will save yourself a lot of time, and your kitchen will always look nice and clean.

I remember when I was a kid living at home. When my mom got through cooking, the kitchen was a mess. Pots, pans, dishes, and anything else she used were in a pile on the counter or in the sink. When we finished eating, all of the plates and eating utensils were added to the pile. This made the kitchen a real mess to clean up after dinner.

One of the smart things that she did after we got an automatic dishwasher was make all of us pick up our plates, glasses, and eating utensils from the table, rinse them off, and then put them into the dishwasher. Then all that was left to clean up were the dirty and sticky pots and pans.

As a waiter in college, I learned to immediately run hot water and perhaps a bit of liquid soap into any pot, pan, or other cooking equipment as soon as I finished using it. If it is allowed to set and cool off, the food and grease become very difficult to clean. I know that this is difficult to do sometimes when you are cooking a big meal, but it makes the job a lot easier in the long run.

To clean my kitchen, I first need to get rid of all the items that I left on the counter when I came into the house from my car. That means letters and other items pertaining to work go to the office and dirty clothes go into the clothes hamper. Yes, I have to hang clean clothes up or fold them and put them away so I don't mess up what I have already done. (I'm picking up a little common sense along the way.) Some items even need to go into the garage.

With the items put away, I tackle the spices, condiments, and other articles left on the counter from cooking dinner last night and put them away. Since I didn't put the clean dishes away, I have to clean out the dishwasher so I can put in the dirty dishes from last night. Once I have everything out of the kitchen that doesn't belong there, I can begin my job.

It is the same routine all over again. I dust high and clean off any smudge marks on the cabinet doors and then clean the counters. Here I use 409 because it is so useful and cuts grease so well. I clean the countertops, the top of the stove, the oven door, the microwave door, the clocks, and the buttons to turn on and off the equipment. After I finish the top of the stove, I always take a look at it from an angle to make sure that there aren't any grease marks or stains on it.

Time-Out

The first time my mother came to visit, she opened the oven door and then laughed. I asked her what was so funny, and she replied, "It doesn't even look like you have ever used it!" Her oven always looked like a pie had exploded in it! (When I use the oven, I always place tin foil under whatever I am cooking so it doesn't fall on the floor of the oven. If something splashes in the oven while I'm cooking, I try to clean it off before its get cold and hardens.)

Back to the Game

After I dust the top of the refrigerator, I use 409 on the door and dry it well. With that move, I am done with the cabinets, counters, and appliances.

Next is vacuuming and then washing the floor. I use the kitchen sink as the bucket. Yep! This is tile, which calls for the Cuban rag mop and VDW. The rag mop is really great because I can put a lot of pressure on the handle to mop up the bad spots, and the cross dowel is small enough to slide under the cabinets, so I don't have to get on my hands and knees to clean under it.

With that done, all I have to do is rinse the rag, clean the sink, and wipe up my tracks as I back out of the kitchen.

My final move is to scout around the whole house and check to see that I haven't overlooked anything. If everything is in tip-top shape, I can take off my helmet and shoulder pads and mark up another victory

* * * * * * *

Now you know how I learned what I know. I have taken all of this information and developed a playbook that you can use to clean your house.

The next section is the actual playbook. Hopefully it will be helpful to you in your house cleaning chores.

THE PLAYBOOK

Introduction

Cleaning a house is much like playing a sport. Learning the proper techniques can make you a much better player or house cleaner. By utilizing the series and plays articulated in this section, you can clean your house in a quicker, more efficient, and more professional manner. Just read and execute. That's all there is to it.

The game of housecleaning consists of scouting, picking up, dusting, cleaning glass and mirrors, and cleaning floors. When you have finished this playbook, you will know the following:

- what you need to do to win the house cleaning game
- how to execute
- proper sequence
- equipment needed
- where to begin and finish

Steps to Achieve Success

Expect to run the full sequence in every room you clean and always execute them in the following order:

1. Scouting
2. Picking up and putting away

3. Dusting
4. Cleaning glass and mirrors
5. Cleaning floors

The reason for doing them in this order is to eliminate the chance of disturbing work that you have already completed. You may have to dry off a tabletop or other piece of furniture under a mirror where you have already dusted. But that is a lot easier than cleaning up dust that has gotten wet from cleaning the mirror or picture above it first.

The benefits of running in the same order every time are as follows:

1. You will develop a routine, and the more times you do it, the easier it will become. This results in quicker and higher quality performance. (Remember that in sports you practice five days a week and play the game once. Practice, practice, practice.)
2. If you have to stop for some reason, it is easier to remember where you left off and resume your route.

When you jump around the room, doing one job and then the other, you invariably will miss something or duplicate work. *Follow the playbook.*

Beginning

At this point you come to a "the chicken or the egg" situation. If you know what you are going to clean, you can begin your scouting now. If you aren't sure, you need to make a preliminary scouting trip so you can decide exactly what you want to clean. Then you can decide where you will start and where you will finish. (Remember to gather all your cleaning gear together before you start so you don't have to stop and look for it when you need it.)

You may decide to do the whole house at one time, or you may decide to break the job up into sections and do some now and some another time. Once you have decided that, you are ready to decide where to start.

If you are doing the whole house, it is better to begin at the room farthest from the exit point and work backward through the house to the exit point, cleaning the rooms as you pass through them. Probably the best place to end your cleaning is the kitchen or the door to the garage.

Kitchens and bathrooms have their own special series, which are located at the end of the floor section.

SCOUTING

What You Will Need

- sharp eyes to find what you are looking for
- possibly a pad and pen to write down discrepancies that need special attention or things that are out of the ordinary

Execution

Always begin at the same point. To be specific, begin at the left side of the door you plan to exit when the room is completed. If necessary, write down the problems.

- Always work in a clockwise direction.
- Check everything out from the ceiling to the floor.
- If you need to write it down to remember it, do it.
- Once you review the execution parts of all of the series, you will know more about what to look for.

PICKING UP AND PUTTING AWAY

What You Will Need

- your hands and rubber gloves
- garbage bags
- hangers

Execution

Walk the proposed path you intend to follow and pick up whatever is out of place and place it where it belongs or remove it completely. Empty trash cans. Return any pillows and other articles to their proper locations.

Picking up and putting away will make it a lot easier to do the rest of the series, and the house will start to look cleaner

DUSTING

What You Will Need

- lint-free cloth or towel
- several microfiber cloths
- furniture spray
- vacuum with hose and attachments (e.g., dust brush, crevice tool, wand, bare floor, and fourteen-inch-wide brush)
- microfiber duster
- cobweb brush with extension handle
- microfiber ceiling fan duster with extension handle
- ladder

Execution

In the navy they have a saying, "If it moves, salute it. If it doesn't, paint it." In housecleaning, we say, "If it has dust on it, dust it."

Remember the clockwise route around the room. Start high and finish low. Remember the law of gravity.

Ceiling Level

Look for dust on ceiling fans, light fixtures, AC registers, molding, and anything else. Most of these won't need to be done every time, but check them on your scouting series until you determine a schedule for dusting them. If you have a bed or other furniture beneath the fan, light fixture, or other ceiling objects, cover them with a sheet or drop cloth.

Eye Level

Check mirrors, pictures, and anything else that might collect dust. Be sure to dust anything that is glass and needs to be cleaned because it will make your cleaning job easier. Also, don't forget to dust the windowsills, door frames, and panels in the doors.

Floor Level

Inspect all furniture and anything that may have dust on it. Remember to check lamps, shades, and especially under the shades and the base of floor lamps. People often neglect these items.

Be sure to dust the rungs on the chairs, between rungs, legs of furniture, statues, and anything else that might collect dust. Also check behind books on tables with shelves and periodically books in bookcases. Use a vacuum attachment with a brush on the books.

By all means, don't forget the flat-screen TV and other sound equipment. On the flat screen follow directions for dusting. Usually it is just water and a special microfiber cloth. Be careful with the cloth. Don't rub hard, and make sure the cloth is made for cleaning flat-screens because they can scratch easily. Follow manufacturer's recommendations if you still have them.

Once you have dusted everything, make a quick pass back over your work again to make sure you didn't miss anything. In football there is always a coach watching to make sure the player does his assignment correctly. How does it feel to be a player coach?

If you are doing a bathroom, go to "Special Bathroom Series" at the end of the floors section and then return here to learn about glasses and mirrors for other rooms.

CLEANING GLASS AND MIRRORS

What You Will Need

- spray bottle with a quarter cup of vinegar and a light squirt of Dawn in a gallon of water
- sponge or lint-free rag
- microfiber rags, towels, old newspapers, or paper towels
- squeegee with extension if needed
- ladder or high step stool
- perhaps a razor blade

Execution

Remember to run the clockwise route around the room and then check anything in the middle of the room.

Check all mirrors, pictures, and anything else on the walls. If dirty or blemished, spray, wash, and then dry them with squeegee, microfiber cloth, newspaper, or paper towel. Be sure to check and see see if there are any wet spots on furniture or floor below where you sprayed. If there are, dry them so that you don't leave spots or damage furniture.

For tables and other flat glass, remove any objects, spray, wash, dry, and replace objects. For lamps that need to be washed, do them first and then pick them up and wash and dry where they sit before you return them. If they are heavy, slide them to the side, clean, and put them back. That makes it look professional because it doesn't look like you simply dusted around the object.

When you come to a window, check and see if it is clean. If so, move on. If dirty, spray, wash, and then dry. For double-hung windows, spray the top windows, wash, and then dry. Then do the ones below. Remember to dry the windowsill if it needs it. Large windows, mirrors, and sliding glass doors are easier to clean if you have a wide sponge and bucket of VDW. Apply VDW with sponge on handle, wash, and then dry with squeegee or microfiber cloth. If you use a squeegee, make sure to overlap the strokes so as to not leave streaks. Also dry the squeegee after each stroke.

To finish, wipe dry any liquid on the glass and then remember to check and dry the sill or floor.

After you wash a glass table or window and want to make sure it is really clean, run the palm of your hand across it. Many times you can feel spots that you can't see. And when you are finished drying a mirror or piece of glass, look at the glass from an angle, and you may see blemishes or streaks that you did not see looking directly at it.

CLEANING THE FLOOR

CARPET

What You Will Need

- vacuum cleaner, either type—upright with hose and attachments or canister with a hose and attachments
- shop vac "for the real man"
- bare floor, crevice, and furniture attachments
- broom and dustpan (just in case you need them)

Note: In either case, your vacuum should have a beater bar on it. That is the bar that rotates and alternates bar and brush on it. Do not use the beater on tile or wood unless you adjust it so that it doesn't hit the floor.

Execution

Vacuum the whole house or each room as you finish it. (Make sure your collection bag has plenty of room for what you are vacuuming and the filter in the sweeper is clean.)

Start in the back of the room farthest from your finish or exit door. Work backward to your goal or goal line so you don't leave tracks on the cleanly vacuumed carpet. (I always think of the Indians covering their tracks in old western movies.)

Move dining room chairs and similar objects rather than vacuuming around or between them.

When necessary make several strokes to clean the carpet. Always overlap your strokes.

On plush carpet where your vacuum leaves marks, try to make them look neat rather than crisscrossing trails. If you are artistic, make a pattern like people do on football fields.

Don't forget the fabric on the furniture. Many people do not realize that the fabric on the furniture also collects dust and should be vacuumed. Use the eight-inch-wide attachment or dust brush. Make sure the attachment doesn't have a beater bar on it.

You can vacuum the fabric on the seats, armrests, and backs of chairs, couches, and any other fabric on furniture. Use the hose attachment with short bristles.

TILE

What You Will Need

- vacuum with hose and attachments without a beater bar
- dust buster or broom and dustpan
- Cuban rag mop or mop of your choosing
- solution of VDW consisting of one cup of vinegar and a squirt of Dawn dishwashing soap per each gallon of water
- couple of rags for drying

Note: A shop vac works great on tile and hardwood floors.

Execution

Vacuum the floor.

If you have the hose and attachment, you can get under almost all furniture. That gets rid of the dust balls.

Move small furniture like dining room chairs and other small objects and vacuum under them rather and then around them.

Mop the floor.

Here's where the choice of equipment is very important and why I like the Cuban rag mop. It consists of a mop handle with T and a rag about the size of half a bath towel. (Google the Cuban rag mop, and you will find all that you need to know about it. Once you have tried it, you will never change.)

If you are mopping the whole house, you can either drag a bucket around or use sinks or clean toilet bowls in the areas you are mopping. This method is quick and easy. Plus you can always have clean water.

Just squirt a little VDW in the toilet. Flush it down when it gets dirty and reload.

Don't forget to back up while mopping so you don't step on the clean floor you have just mopped.

Wood and Laminate

What You Will Need

- vacuum and attachment *without beater bar*
- dust mop
- wax/polish, oil soaps, or other cleaners (for wood only)

Note: Make sure the wheels of the vacuum are soft and smooth and free of debris. Do not use wet mop on wood floors.

Execution

Vacuum and/or dust. It is your choice. (If manufacturer's recommendations are different, follow them.)

Marble

What You Will Need

- vacuum with hose and attachments without a beater bar
- dust mop or soft bristle broom

- mild liquid soap
- Cuban rag mop or mop of your choosing
- warm water, ideally distilled or as close to neutral pH as possible
- bucket
- couple of rags for drying

Note: A shop vac works great on tile and hardwood floors.

Execution

Do not use any solution that contains acid. That includes vinegar, lemon juice, or items like ammonia and tile cleaner. It should be dusted frequently and cleaned with a damp cloth by hand or mop. If it needs to be washed, use a mild soap, rinse well, and wipe dry. The frequency depends on how quickly it gets dirty, dusty, or soiled.

For more detailed care, consult your hardware store or installation company, or you can google your options. There are many excellent cleaning liquids. I am by no means an expert.

BATHROOM

What You Will Need

You will need equipment for picking up, dusting, cleaning glass and mirrors, and cleaning the floor. You will also need these additional items:

- toilet brush
- scrub brush or course sponge
- VDW, Soft Scrub, and tile and bath cleaner
- towels or rags for drying
- Cuban rag mop or your selection
- bucket

Note: You can use the toilet as a bucket or bring your own.

Execution

Complete the standard steps within all the series.

Next vacuum with hose and attachments or sweep the floor, shower floor, bottom of bathtub, and any other horizontal places, including the windowsills and the ledge around the bathtub. This will make cleaning them a lot easier.

Then with VDW, Soft Scrub, or bath and tile cleaner, clean the shower, tub, sink, counter, and finally the toilet. *Do not use VDW, ammonia, tile cleaner, or anything with acid on either marble or granite.* See below for tips on both.

The shower enclosure

- With VDW or tile and bath cleaner, spray the shower wall, floor, and any glass within the shower enclosure and let set. If you have mold, spray it with a solution of concentrated Clorox and water (one cup of Clorox with three cups of water). Wipe metal fixtures quickly so they don't get pitted by the cleaners. If your shower walls and floor are marble, don't use anything acidic like vinegar, lemon juice, ammonia, or tile cleaner. Consult Google or reliable marble stores for products to clean with.

- Clean everything in the shower enclosure. You may need a scrub brush or rough sponge to get bad areas. Rinse well and then dry with rag and squeegee.

The rest of the bathroom

- Spray the tub and any tile around it, the sink, countertop (if tile), and the entire toilet. Immediately rinse and dry metal fixtures.
- Prioritize the dirtiness of what you are going to clean and then start cleaning the cleanest one first and work in reverse, leaving the dirtiest one last. That should be the toilet. You do this to allow the cleaning agent to work on the dirtier items.
- Clean and rinse sink and countertop, tile around the tub, the tub, and the toilet.
- When you wash the toilet, start at the tank's top, seat, outside of the toilet, including the base and behind the toilet, and then finally address the lip and inside the toilet bowl last. Rinse and dry in the same order.

If the floor or the bottom of the tub or shower is really bad, take a rag and use your foot to push the rag around. You can get a lot of pressure that way. Just be careful and don't bust your ass.

Be sure to rinse thoroughly and dry any metal fixtures and metal frames to prevent pitting from the chemicals

The last task is cleaning the floor. If you didn't vacuum the floor earlier, do it now. After you clean the toilet, you can use it as your bucket and save some time and effort. Pour into the toilet a cup of vinegar and a squirt of Dawn, and you have your VDW. If the water gets dirty, simply flush it down, and you have clean water to rinse the floor. Wash the floor with the Cuban rag mop or your choice of mop. You will probably have to get on your knees and use a rag to get the floor behind the toilet.

Once you are done, dry off the toilet and floor around it. Make sure everything is copasetic, pick up your tools, and move on to the next room.

While cleaning, I also found the toilet convenient to wash out the wastebasket.

If the shower curtain is dirty, remove it and all its hooks and then throw the curtain in the washer with some towels and add vinegar and laundry soap. Wash on gentle cycle and warm water and then remove it immediately and hang it up. The wrinkles should drop out of it, and you will have a clean shower curtain.

With marble, wipe up any spills immediately. To clean, wipe with clean, soft towel. Clean with water that has a low pH or mild soap if necessary, rinse well, and then dry with soft cloth. Google how to clean marble for more information or consult hardware stores on their products.

With granite, wipe up with clean white cloth. Microfiber is also good. Wash with liquid dish soap, rinse well, and dry with clean, soft cloth. Google how to clean granite for more information or consult hardware stores on their products.

THE KITCHEN

What You Will Need

Make sure you have all supplies and equipment for the first four series plus the following for the kitchen:

- WD-40
- 409

Execution

Run the first four series like all other rooms. If you have done them correctly, you will have picked everything up and put them in their proper places, dusted, cleaned the cabinet tops and fronts, dusted the top of the refrigerator, and possibly dusted even the decorations above the cabinets. The counters should be free of everything as much as possible.

Special things you should be aware of in cleaning the kitchen

Check for smudges and handprints on the cabinets and counter. Clean with VDW or 409. These two cleaners should clean everything in the kitchen.

Clean all small appliances. This includes the coffeepot, toaster, and any other small appliance.

Clean the front of the refrigerator, stove, and dishwasher. For stainless steel appliances and the kitchen sink, use WD-40. When you are using WD-40, spray it on and then be sure to wipe it dry. Keep polishing it until you have a nice even luster. Any smell should go away quickly.

Sometimes it works best to spray the WD-40 on the rag and then wipe the object. That saves getting spray all over the place.

For modern glass-top stoves you can clean them with VDW, 409, or soft scrub, or better yet, buy the cleaner recommended by the manufacturer.

For microwave fronts, key pads, and just about anything else, try VDW. I like 409 because it is mild, doesn't harm anything, and cuts grease well. Don't forget underneath the microwave overhang area.

Next to last you have the kitchen counter. Depending on how dirty it is, use soap and water, VDW, or 409. Sometimes you may need bleach to clean up some stains. Take a towel and dry it off and make sure it is all clean.

If you are going to use the sink for your water supply to wash the floor, run water in both sinks. Add a quarter of a cup of vinegar and a squirt of Dawn to each gallon of water in the first sink. Run only water in the other sink to rinse out your rag. (If the sink is granite, do not put vinegar in it. Use a bucket.)

To save time and make it easier, use the Cuban rag mop. Mop underneath the overhang of the cabinets and on the sides the refrigerator and stove, making sure to clean the corners. Pull the stove and refrigerator out and vacuum and then mop behind them every three months.

Always rinse the rag or mop in the clean water before you dip it into the VDW water in the other sink. If you want to rinse after you wash, drain the sinks and refill one of them.

If this your last room and exit point, it is time to go back through the whole house and make sure everything is looking great.

Once you are satisfied with your job, stow your gear, remove your helmet, and celebrate the victory with a cold frosty beer.

Cheers!

You are finally prepared to go out and lead your team to victory in the housecleaning game. There is one final thing you need. You have noticed that a lot of quarterbacks wear a wristband that has the important plays listed on them. In the following section are the four important plays that will handle almost every situation you may encounter.

SPECIAL PLAYS

Important Plays
for Special Situations

As the quarterback, you may change any of them even when you are up to the line and ready to start the play. The important point is that all of the movements are included so you know what to do in each situation. They are as follows:

- **Fullback up the Middle**—This play is your normal biweekly cleanup. How dirty or messed up your house gets or how neat you are will determine how frequently you will run this play.
- **The Full Monty**—This play is to be used when you want to do a spring housecleaning or as the pros call it, "a deep clean."
- **Quarterback Sneak**—This play is for the times when you know someone is coming to visit you and the place is in pretty good shape. However, once you have learned the system, you will probably run this play in place of the "Fullback up the Middle" because you want to slack off. Just remember that every time you slack off, the next time you clean the job will be more difficult.
- **Hail Mary**—Run this play when someone knocks on your door and you have your jock strap around your knees. In other words, they have caught you unexpectedly off guard!

Special Plays in Detail

FULLBACK UP THE MIDDLE

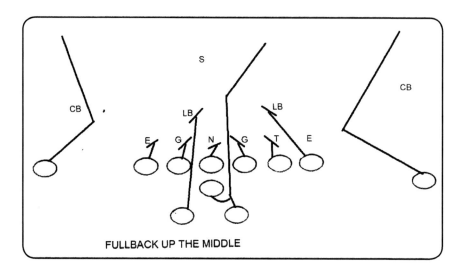

FULLBACK UP THE MIDDLE

Normal Housecleaning

This is your normal housecleaning play. Run it about every two weeks. The time between cleanings will depend on how fast your home accumulates dust and how neat you keep it. Dust is usually the deciding factor.

The more stuff you have to move around when you clean, the longer it is going to take. Moving clutter wastes time. So if you can think of the objects around your house that are not really important, think about storing them or getting rid of them.

Scouting

No matter how good you think you are, it is always best to scout around your house to see exactly what has to be done. That's why football teams have scouts. It is a lot better to head into a job, knowing what you are going to encounter rather than being surprised at the last minute. It also helps you know exactly what equipment you are going to need to do your job.

Cleanup and Prep

First of all, regardless of what cleaning play you are going to run, you need to remove all the items that don't belong there and put them away. If you are a person who hangs up your clothes after you take them off or put them in the hamper, this job is going to be a lot easier to do.

Dusting

Start high and finish low. Remember the law of gravity. If you have anything underneath a fan, light fixture, or anything else, remember to spread a sheet or drop cloth over whatever is below. You might have moldings, high pictures, or even a moose head. Dust them if they need it. The dusting tool list has whatever you need.

Proceed clockwise around the room, dusting anything that has dust on it. Don't forget the part of the furniture below the cushion. If you have windows, don't forget the sills and frames of the windows. Lots of people forget them. Be sure and dust any glass that has dust because it will make it easier to wash. Sometimes dusting may be all it needs.

Once you have completed your dusting task, take a look and see if you have missed anything. In sports there is always a coach watching to make sure the player does his assignment correctly. In cleanup it is punch-out time! You are your own punch-out man!

Once you have completed the dusting, you are ready for glass and mirrors.

Glass and Mirrors

Follow the same clockwise route as you did when you dusted. Use VDW or a Windex substitute. Check all mirrors, glass, and anything else. If you do a mirror that has something below it, check to make sure some of the mist hasn't spotted it. If so, dry it off. This is one of the few times that you might have to do a job twice. Remember, it is easier to clean up if there is no dust for the mist to fall on.

When you come to a window, check to see if it's clean. If it is, move on.

If it's small, the spray bottle of VDW should suffice. Spray and wash with a cloth, brush, sponge, or even your hand. (Lots of times human touch detects things that the eye cannot see.) Squeegee it and clean up the edges with a microfiber rag or old newspaper.

If it's a large piece of glass like a sliding glass door, you may need a bucket and wide sponge on a handle to wash it clean. A squeegee works great to dry it. Don't forget to dry around the edge with microfiber, a lint-free rag, or even a newspaper.

Once you are finished, retrace your steps and look at your work. Check for streaks or blemishes on the mirrors, windows, or anything else you have cleaned. (If you look at the glass or mirror from an angle, you can sometimes see streaks that you don't see looking head-on.)

Special Tasks before the Floor in Bedroom, Man Cave, Bath, and Kitchen

Bedroom

Unless you changed the bed when you got up this morning, now is the time to do it plus any other final jobs you need to do to clean the room.

The Man Cave

Some men have them, so we can't leave them out. The cave is your own special place. Follow the same procedure as normal rooms. I can't tell you what to do, but I can leave you with the thought that the less amount of trophies, certificates, pictures of you and Tom Brady, and anything else you may have to move in order to dust, the easier it is to clean.

Bathroom

Clean the toilet, shower, tub, sink, and anything else before you do the floor. If you have cleaned the toilet, using it as your bucket will save bringing in a bucket and taking the chance of spilling it all over the floor. Simply pour in a solution of a cup of vinegar and a squirt of Dawn, and you have your VDW. You can use it to wash the floor without risking spilling the bucket. When it gets dirty, simply flush it, and you have a clean water to rinse the floor if you are so inclined. I also found it handy to wash out the wastebasket when it gets dirty.

Kitchen

Don't forget the top of the refrigerator and cabinets and any decorative items. If you have a toaster and coffeemaker, now is the time to do them along with the front of the stove and oven. Clean up spots under the microwave, the keypad, the face of the microwave, the dishwasher, the oven doors, and anything else you can think of that are often missed.

Besides VDW, I use a lot of 409 because it cuts grease and cleans almost everything with a minimum of effort.

Before I clean the sink, I fill one side with VDW solution and rinse the rag mop in the other side as I do the floor. Again there's no need for the bucket, and you can let the remains go down the drain. You might also think of cleaning the garbage can if it isn't too messy before you drain the sink.

For this task only, clean the floor and then finish the kitchen by cleaning the sink. If the sink and appliances are stainless steel, WD-40 is a great way to clean these. It is supposed to be harmless, but I wouldn't drink it. Simply spray and then wipe very well. Everything should come off, and you end up with a nice shine to it. The smell disappears quickly.

The Floor

This is the final movement.

Carpet

For carpet I prefer the upright with hose attachments because I can push it around in the open area and use the hose and attachments for under and behind the furniture. Either one works well.

I prefer to start in the back of the room and back myself to the exit door, trying to leave even marks on the carpet.

Fabric on furniture

People often don't think about the fabric on the furniture. It gets dirty also and needs vacuuming as much as the carpet. Try to remember to vacuum the cushions, the arms, and the back of the chairs and couches. Just vacuum and don't use an attachment with a beater bar.

Tile and synthetic floors

Vacuum first and then follow up with a Cuban rag mop or your choice of mop and a solution of VDW either in a bucket or a nearby clean toilet or sink. Back your way to the exit door.

Wood and laminate

Wood and laminate floors will show signs of wear over time, and regular cleaning and maintenance are necessary. The following steps are recommended.

1. Vacuum, sweep, or dust-mop regularly. Make sure the vacuum has soft wheels and is free of dirt and other debris. Do not use a vacuum with a beater bar head. The beater bar is that thing that rotates around under your vacuum sweeper and is supposed to beat the dust out of your carpet.
2. Remove spills promptly with a soft, clean cloth, a damp cloth with water, and soap if necessary. Rinse and dry.
3. Never use wax/polish, wet-mop, oil soaps, or cleaners like Pledge, etc. Use only cleaners recommended for hardwoods.
4. Dirt and sand can scratch and dull the floor. Use floor mats at the entrances. Use a rug in high traffic areas. Do not use plastic/vinyl mats on wood floors as they will trap the moisture in the floor and rot the wood.
5. Use protective felt pads on the bottom of furniture legs so they don't scratch the floor. Some people even use old tennis balls in informal areas.
6. Sunlight may discolor wood so you should either have shades, shutters, or solar film to protect the wood.
7. Keep pets' nails trimmed and paws clean and free of gravel and other abrasive items.

Here's the final punch out. Once you are done with the floors, the only task left to do is to go back and take a look at everything to make sure it all looks good. Many times when you step away from work and then go back to take a look, you notice things you missed. Fix them and then take off your helmet, shoulder pads, and cleats because you have won the game.

THE FULL MONTY

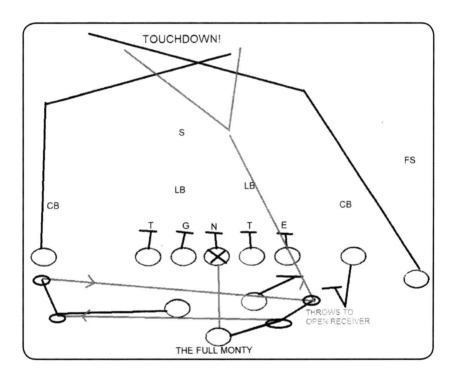

THE FULL MONTY

Spring Housecleaning or Semiannual Cleanup

This play is for when you want to do a complete housecleaning. The cleaning professionals call it a deep clean. This time you are going to need all of your cleaning supplies, so you might as well put them beside the bench and be ready to go in and play.

Always remember the series—scout, pick up, dust, glass and mirrors, and floor. You will do this in every room, only it will be more detailed and complete.

After doing your scouting of the whole job, you may decide to split the effort into segments or quarters and complete the job over a period of days.

1. **Scout**—This time you are going to have to look closer because we are getting into detail, so you really need to pay attention and possibly take notes along the way.

2. **Dust**—Get your ladder out because you will be taking a close look at everything on the ceiling and above normal reach. While you are up there, if needed, clean the chandelier and anything else included in the section on glass and mirrors. Follow the procedure and don't forget to check everything closely.

3. **Glass and Mirrors**—Follow normal procedure here with a sharp eye!

4. **The Floor**

- **Carpet**: Check high traffic areas for excess dirt. It may be time to get your carpet cleaned.

- **Tile**: You may need to use the toothbrush and bleach for the grout in some places. Otherwise, follow normal procedure for this series.

Scouting and Prep	Dusting	Glass and Mirrors	Floors
	Up high		
Look around everywhere	Ceiling corners	Anything shiny	Under beds
Pick up	Molding	Figurines	Under other furniture
Put away	Ceiling fans	Windows	Behind furniture
Throw out	Light fixtures	Mirrors	Heavy traffic areas
	Middle level	Tabletop	Behind doors
	Lamps, including bulbs, shades, etc.	Flat screen TV	
	Figurines		
	Furniture		
	Behind furniture		
	TV and radio		
	Pictures		
	Base of floor lamps		
	Rungs on chairs		
	Magazine racks		
	Anything else with dust on it		

QUARTERBACK SNEAK

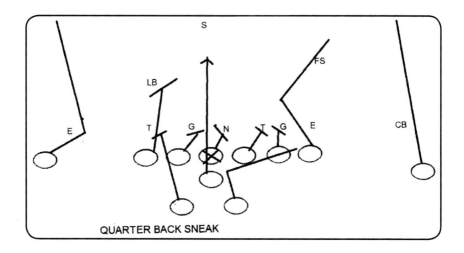

QUARTER BACK SNEAK

Quick Cleanup

This play is for when you need a quick cleanup because an unexpected guest is coming over or you are just too lazy to do the complete job in the first place. You can use it for one room or the whole house.

Always use the basic plan first and foremost.

1. **Scout and Pick up**—You need sharp eyes and quick hands. Look around the room. Pick up and put away what doesn't belong there. Look high and around windows for dust or cobwebs. If you don't see anything, go to the next step.

2. **Dust**—You need two microfiber dust rags, one for each hand. You may need furniture spray and possibly a microfiber feather duster or long-haired brush. Dust in a clockwise direction around the room, dusting all furniture flat areas

and anywhere else that shows dust, such as windowsills and tabletops. Then dust anything in the middle. Check mirrors and other areas to see if they have streaks or spots. If you can get away with just wiping dust off the mirrors and flat areas, do it. Maybe you can even skip glass cleaning.

3. **Glass and Mirrors**—You need a cleaning rag, a microfiber drying rag, VDW in a spray bottle, and possibly a squeegee. Be sure and check for smears and blemishes when you are finished and make sure furniture below isn't spotted from spray.

4. **Floor**—For carpet you will need a vacuum and possibly a broom and dustpan. For tile you need a vacuum and possibly a Cuban rag mop and VDW. Start at the back of the room and work your way toward the exit so you don't mess up what you just completed. Just make it look good. If the floor is clean and shined, you might be able to skip the mopping.

5. **Bathroom**—Check to see that you have clean towels and that the sink and counter are clean. Most importantly, check the toilet to see that it is clean and doesn't have any alligators crawling around in the bowl. *Check the toilet seat.* If you are a pointer and pee like a man, make sure the toilet seat doesn't have any spots on it! Also check for splatter marks on the floor near the toilet.

If you do it in this order you probably will not have to do anything twice and can meet your guests on time. As a final step, you can greet guests with a big smile, handshake or hug, and a drink.

THE HAIL MARY PLAY

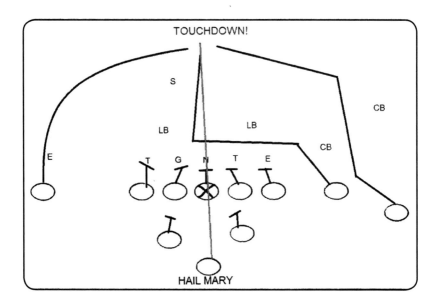

When There Is No Time Left in the Game

This play is for when there is no hope of getting the place cleaned up at all because guests unexpectedly have showed up at your door.

1. Greet the guests at the front door with a big smile and a fresh drink in your hand.
2. Give each a big hug and hearty greeting without spilling your drink on them. (Maybe you should put it down.)
3. Invite them in, offer them drinks, and keep smiling and talking. Try to avoid the really bad areas in the house. Maybe they won't notice. This is when charm really counts!

Good luck and happy cleaning!

Good Luck and Clean Like a Pro!

CPSIA information can be obtained at www.ICGtesting.com
Printed in the USA
LVOW07s0108160215

427175LV00001B/113/P